28

JESUS CENTERED

YOUTH GROUP

DEVOTIONS

PROVEN IMPACT WITH 100,000+ TEENAGERS

28 Jesus-Centered Youth Group Devotions
Copyright © 2016 Group Publishing, Inc. / 0000 0001 0362 4853

group.com
simplyyouthministry.com

Credits
Executive Developer: Tim Gilmour
Executive Editor: Rick Lawrence
Chief Creative Officer: Joani Schultz
Editor: Stephanie Martin
Art Director and Cover Art: Veronica Preston
Production: Veronica Preston
Project Manager: Justin Boling

Any website addresses included in this book are offered only as a resource and/or reference for the reader. The inclusion of these websites is not intended, in any way, to be interpreted as an endorsement of these sites or their content on the part of Group Publishing or the author. In addition, the author and Group Publishing do not vouch for the content of these websites for the life of this book.

Unless otherwise indicated, all Scripture quotations are taken from the New Living Translation, copyright © 1996, 2004, 2007. Used by permission of Tyndale House Publishers, Inc., Carol Stream, Illinois 60188. All rights reserved.

ISBN 978-1-4707-4288-1
10 9 8 7 6 5 4 3 2 1   21 20 19 18 17 16

Printed in the United States of America.

TABLE OF CONTENTS

28

JESUS
CENTERED

YOUTH
GROUP
DEVOTIONS

PROVEN IMPACT WITH 100,000+ TEENAGERS

INTRODUCTION

If we choose the *right* habit to change in our life, we can end up changing *all* of our habits...for the better. In Charles Duhigg's book *The Power of Habit*, he calls that one *right* habit the "keystone habit." He says: "The habits that matter most are the ones that, when they start to shift, dislodge and remake other patterns." So, what's your "keystone habit" related to helping teenagers grow spiritually? I mean, what are your underlying assumptions when you're trying to help kids mature in their faith? Fill in the blanks here: "Because I _____, I expect my students to _____."

Whatever words fill those blanks, they represent your youth ministry *orthopraxy*—the way you *practice* what you believe about spiritual growth. These 28 youth group devotions are designed to help you *practice* a profound and transformative habit in your ministry... It's called The Progression, and it goes like this:

"Get to know Jesus well, because the more you know him, the more you'll love him, and the more you love him, the more you'll want to follow him, and the more you follow him, the more you'll become like him, and the more you become like him, the more you become yourself."

When we help students "get to know Jesus well," they develop a deep love for him that compels them to follow him, and they slowly become like him as a result. And somewhere along the way, their "true self"—the "fearfully and wonderfully made" self—emerges into the light. Use these devotions to create or fuel a Jesus-centered habit in your ministry, and that "keystone habit" may just change everything else in your ministry. When your teenagers sense a deep agreement with Paul's declaration from 1 Corinthians 2—"For I determined to know nothing among you except Jesus Christ, and him crucified"—something deep changes in them.

The normal Christian life can feel like an epic everyday adventure when you've been ruined by Jesus and ruined for Jesus.

—Rick Lawrence, Executive Editor

28

JESUS CENTERED

YOUTH
GROUP
DEVOTIONS

PROVEN IMPACT WITH 100,000+ TEENAGERS

SECTION 1:

WHO IS JESUS?

1. DESCRIBING JESUS

Supplies: Bibles, paper, pens or pencils

quiet, Sometimes organized, hardworking

✳ SAY Think of three words to describe yourself. (Allow time.) Now think of three words to describe Jesus. (Allow time.)

Loving, all knowing, Caring

✳ ASK Which was more difficult: describing yourself in three words or describing Jesus in three words? Explain.

Have students share some words that describe Jesus.

✳ ASK Of all the words you've heard that describe Jesus, which was the most interesting? the most surprising? Over time, how have your thoughts about Jesus changed? What's different between then and now? Do you think Jesus' view of you has changed over time? How so?

✳ Have students take turns reading aloud Philippians 2:5-8.

✳ ASK What words does this Bible passage use to describe Jesus? Did any of you have those words on your list? Why or why not?

✳ SAY Getting close to Jesus is an incredible experience, but it may not always be what you expect. Even if you've known Jesus your whole life, you may be missing out on some aspects of who he really is. The more time you spend with Jesus and in his Word, the more opportunities he'll have to show you who he really is, what he really thinks of you, and what his plans are for your life.

SAY Let's close in prayer. Turn to a person near you and take one minute each to pray for the other person. Pray that Jesus will make himself real to your partner and will continue speaking words of love to them. You'll have about two minutes.

Allow time for prayer.

2. PICTURING JESUS

Supplies: Bibles

SAY As followers of Jesus, we have the opportunity to see him in a new way—and also to learn some new things about ourselves. By reframing the way we see Jesus, we can also see ourselves in a new light. Let's experience what that can look like for us.

SAY Close your eyes. While I tell you a brief story, imagine you're in a room with a picture of Jesus hanging on the wall.

At a Christian middle school, one person taught sixth grade and the other taught seventh. In the seventh-grade classroom, a copy of an old and very famous portrait of Jesus hung in an ornate frame. The teacher didn't like the picture. She thought it wasn't an accurate depiction of who Jesus really was. So one night she took the picture down, snuck into the sixth-grade classroom, and hung it there. The next morning, the sixth-grade teacher was shocked to find this old picture of Jesus hanging in his room. He didn't think it was an accurate picture either. And he knew where it had come from. So, after everyone had gone home that day, he returned the picture. This started a yearlong battle. Each week or so, one teacher and then the other would find creative places to put that picture in the other teacher's room until one of them finally tucked it away in a closet, never to be seen again.

SAY Open your eyes, turn to a partner, and describe the picture you saw in your mind as I told this story. Give details. What did Jesus look like? What did the frame look like? (Allow time.) Now share with your partner the picture of Jesus that hangs in your mind. What does he look like? How does he behave? What words describe him? (Allow time.)

SAY With your partner, share the way you've pictured Jesus in the past and how that picture of him has changed over time. Tell about something in your life—a person or an experience—that helped you see Jesus differently, more as he really is. Then share how you see Jesus today. (Allow time.)

✳ Have someone read aloud John 14:8-10.

✳ SAY Jesus is truly God. He tells us that when we see him, we see the Father—we see God. That means if we pay much better attention to Jesus—what he really said and did—then we'll come to understand God's heart more deeply. Let's invite Jesus to reframe how we see him, the world, and ourselves.

Close in prayer.

3. LOOKING AT JESUS

Supplies: Bibles

SAY Take a moment to think about all the different things you like to look at. (Pause.) Imagine that today—right now—is the last chance you'll have to look at certain people, places, sights, events, beautiful things, or something else. Think of all the things your eyes have seen, could see, might ever see. What would be your last sight to look at and why?

Allow time for sharing.

SAY What we look at—and how we look at it—says a lot about us. The same goes for Jesus. We all can be looking at him, but what we see depends on how we look.

Have someone read aloud John 19:13-15.

ASK How did the people in this Bible passage look at Jesus? Why did they see him that way?

Have someone read aloud John 20:26-28.

ASK In this passage, how did Thomas and the rest of the disciples look at Jesus? Why did they see him that way?

SAY Jesus was the same in both passages, but people's perspectives were completely different. One group looked and saw a criminal who should be put to death. Another looked and saw the Lord, their God.

ASK When you look at Jesus, what are some things you see? How does looking at Jesus affect your outlook in other areas? For example, how does your view of Jesus change your view about yourself?

SAY Let's close in prayer. Dear Jesus, thank you for never changing. Please help us dig into your Word so we can discover who you really are—and what that means for us. In Jesus' name, amen.

4. NAMING JESUS

Supplies: Bibles, paper, pens or pencils

SAY Names are fascinating, and many of them have special meanings.

ASK How do you feel about your name? Have you ever wanted to go by a different name? If so, explain.

SAY Let's take a few minutes to suggest new names—or nicknames—for one another. Turn to a partner and brainstorm some suggestions related to something good or unique about that person. Ready? Go!

Allow time. Then ask a few students to share their ideas with everyone.

SAY Some people answer to more than just one name. In the Bible, Jesus is called many names in both the Old and New Testaments. Turn to Isaiah 9:6.

Have someone read that verse aloud.

ASK What names for Jesus are listed in this verse? What other names for Jesus can you think of? Which name for Jesus is your favorite, and why? What does it mean to you—and to your faith?

SAY Whether it's "Prince of Peace," "Good Shepherd," "Savior," or another name, what we call Jesus is one way to get to know him better.

SAY Let's get in a circle and close with an open time of prayer, focusing on who Jesus is to each of us. To do that, begin your prayer with these words, "Jesus, you are…" and then finish the sentence. It's okay to pray something very brief, or to not pray at all. We just want to talk to God about who his Son is to us. Anyone can start, and I'll close. Let's pray.

5. RECEIVING JESUS

Supplies: Bibles

Have students take turns reading aloud Jesus' parable of the prodigal son, from Luke 15:11-32.

ASK How do you feel about the father's response to the prodigal son at his homecoming?

SAY Jesus shared this parable so we can know that God the Father wants to respond to us the same way and extend the same undeserved forgiveness—if we'll simply receive it. But we can't do that if our fists are clenched tight.

Have students tighten their fists.

ASK How does it make you feel to clench like this? Using just one word, what are some things you're hanging on to that might prevent you from receiving Jesus and his forgiveness?

Ask if anyone is willing to share their word with the whole group.

ASK How would you describe who Jesus is to you? What has he done—or what could he do—inside your heart? Do you feel as if you deserve anything from Jesus? Why or why not? What, if anything, is keeping you from fully accepting Jesus' love and gifts?

SAY Because of our sins, no one deserves anything from Jesus—except eternal punishment. Thankfully, Jesus came to earth to die for us, making us righteous in God the Father's eyes. Now we can grow in our relationship with Jesus, knowing that he offers us all the forgiveness, love, and grace we'll ever need.

ASK Now that you've received this undeserved good news, how can you respond? How can you live for Jesus? And how can you share his good news with other people?

SAY Let's close in a time of open prayer, with our eyes closed. If you have a new—or renewed—perspective on your relationship with Jesus, offer a simple prayer that begins with, "Jesus, I receive you…" and then fill in the rest of that sentence however you'd like. Details are okay but not necessary. After a little while, I'll close. Let's bow our heads and pray.

Allow plenty of time for this to develop. Don't be afraid of silence.

SECTION 2:

WHAT IS JESUS LIKE?

6. JESUS SEES US

Supplies: Bibles, paper, pens or pencils

SAY Find and face a partner. Extend your right arm and place it on your partner's left shoulder. Then drop your arms and remain that far away from each other. I'll give you 30 seconds to study each other a little. (Give no further instruction. After 30 seconds, continue.)

SAY Now turn back to back, with one of you facing me and the other facing away. I'll ask four questions. The person facing me will answer first, followed by the person facing away. Here we go:

1. What color are your partner's eyes?

2. How much taller or shorter than you is your partner?

3. What kind of shoes is your partner wearing?

4. What jewelry, if any, is your partner wearing?

SAY Now turn around and check your answers. (Pause.) How many of you got every question right? How many missed one? How many missed more than one? (Allow time.)

SAY In a friendship, knowing what your friend looks like is only a very small part of the equation. Now face your partner and tell something you know about him or her that isn't visible, such as a character trait, an interest, or an attitude that makes them special. (Allow time.)

SAY A good friend can know us better than we know ourselves. And that has nothing to do with eye color or physical appearance or what we wear. A true friend sees past all that and sees something in us that maybe even we don't see. A good friend can even help us see who we can be—even if we're not that person right now.

SAY Let's read about an encounter Jesus had with a guy named Nathanael.

Have someone read aloud John 1:48-49.

SAY Jesus sees who we really are long before we see him for who he really is. In fact, Jesus knew you before you were born. Take a few moments now to consider what your friend Jesus likes about you, as well as what you like about Jesus. As words or phrases come to mind, write them on your piece of paper. Let's take two full minutes of silence to think about our friend Jesus. (Allow time.)

Close in prayer.

7. JESUS LOVES US

Supplies: Bibles, a dictionary

[SAY] These days, we don't use the word "prodigal" very often. In fact, the only time many of us hear it is in Jesus' parable of the prodigal son.

Ask someone familiar with that parable to recap it for everyone. Then read the dictionary definitions of prodigal.

[ASK] After hearing that summary and those definitions, how would you define the word prodigal? In what ways would you say you've been prodigal—in good ways, bad ways, or anything in between?

[SAY] Today, let's focus on one person in the parable of the prodigal son—the father. He's a fascinating character because it seems he has endless tolerance, patience, forgiveness, and love for his children. And that's exactly what God the Father has for us, through his Son, Jesus.

Have someone read aloud Ephesians 3:18.

[ASK] When have you felt Jesus' prodigal love like that verse describes? How does it feel to know about Jesus' never-ending love for you, even though you don't deserve it and can't ever do anything to deserve it?

[SAY] Jesus does amazing things in each of our lives. Because of his love and mercy, the words prodigal and undeserved can become part of our faith story and the story of our group.

[SAY] Let's close in prayer. Dear Jesus, thanks for being so "prodigal" in your love toward us. Help us be the same in response to you and to other people. In Jesus' name, amen.

8. JESUS REPAIRS US

Supplies: Bibles, paper, pens or pencils, and something that kids can toss back and forth (a ball, a sock, a lightweight book, etc.)

SAY Take a minute to think about the word "transformation." The dictionary defines it as a change in form, appearance, nature, or character.

SAY Consider all the things, people, events…anything…that can be transformed. I'll start by naming something that can be transformed. Then I'll toss this (hold up your item) to another person. They'll have five seconds to say a new thing that can be transformed, and it can't be a word that's already been said. We'll add pressure by counting down after the item has been tossed. Ready? I'll take an easy one: me.

Toss the item and say, "5, 4, 3, 2, 1." Keep the game moving until everyone has had the item at least once and people are running out of words.

ASK Thinking about what we named, what are some of the easier things to transform? What are the more difficult things? Explain.

SAY Jesus was in the transformation business. Here are two brief, very different stories of transformation he pulled off. In John 2, Jesus is at a wedding, and they run out of wine. At his mother's request, Jesus transforms regular water into excellent-quality wine. Then in Luke 19, Jesus meets Zaccheus, a chief tax collector and all-around cheating scoundrel who's known as a "notorious sinner." Jesus joins him for dinner, and by the end of the night, Zaccheus believes in Jesus.

ASK Which story do you think is a bigger transformation, and why? (Allow time for discussion.)

ASK What is your story with Jesus today? In other words, how did you two meet, and where are you in your relationship right now? Turn to a person sitting next to you, and take a couple of minutes to share your story. There are no right or wrong stories, and you can include or leave out any details you want. (Allow time.)

SAY Your story with Jesus is the most important story you'll ever have. No matter where in the story you are, Jesus has something incredible planned for you.

SAY Let's close our eyes and be still. I'll read a brief prayer, and then let's listen for Jesus' answer. Then, when the minute is up, write down the first word or phrase that comes to mind. Again, there's no right or wrong answer, and it's okay not to know what to expect. Let's just see what Jesus says to each of us.

SAY Please close your eyes, and listen to this prayer: Jesus, you want to repair us...to transform us...to take our story to the next level. Speak to us, Jesus, about how you might want to do that. What do I need to know? What do I need to avoid or set aside to see you more clearly? Will you whisper something to me about how you'll repair me and transform my story?

Allow one minute of silence. Then have everyone write down the first word or phrase that comes to mind. Close by asking if anyone wants to share what they wrote.

9. JESUS LEADS US

Supplies: Bibles

[SAY] You may have heard that Jesus is called our good Shepherd. Guess what that makes us? (Pause.) Yep, Jesus repeatedly describes people as lost sheep in need of help and rescue. Here's one example.

Read Matthew 9:36-37.

[SAY] "Confused and helpless" sheep—really? Listen as I describe what sheep are like, and think about how these descriptions might ring true for us. If you hear something that reminds you of what we're actually like, give a loud "Baaaa!"

- Timid, fearful, and easily panicked
- Typically stupid and gullible
- Vulnerable to fear, frustration, pests, and hunger
- Easily influenced by a strong, calm leader
- Easily prodded into a stampede; vulnerable to a "mob mentality"
- Have little or no means of self-defense; easily killed by their enemies
- Jealous and competitive for dominance
- Always seeking fresh water and fresh pastures but not very discerning in their choices
- Stubborn and always insisting on their own way
- Easily tipped over onto their back and unable to right themselves
- Bothered by someone who tries to clean or shear their wool
- Creatures of habit that often get stuck in "ruts"
- Needy; they require more care than any other livestock

SAY Now turn to a partner and discuss this question: What one or two of these "sheepy" descriptions fits you pretty well? (Allow two minutes.)

SAY It's hard to admit that Jesus compares us to this embarrassing animal. But let's listen to the Bible passage again, this time paying close attention to Jesus' heart toward the sheep.

Re-read Matthew 9:36-37.

SAY Return to your partner and discuss this question: If this Bible passage were the only evidence you had of Jesus' heart toward you, what would you know for sure about him? (Allow two minutes.)

ASK What are some things you know for sure about Jesus, based only on this passage?

SAY The deepest truth about Jesus' heart toward us is summed up in the children's song "Jesus Loves Me." Let's sing the first part together: Jesus loves me, this I know, for the Bible tells me so. Little ones to him belong, they are weak but he is strong. Yes, Jesus loves me. Yes, Jesus loves me. Yes, Jesus loves me, the Bible tells me so.

SAY Jesus wants to be our Shepherd because he loves us so much. It's okay to admit "we are weak, but he is strong." As sheep, we don't need to work harder to get stronger. We just need to respond to our good Shepherd's offer to have us for his own. If we learn to trust Jesus, he'll look out for us, defend us, and rescue us. Let's take a moment of silence to talk to Jesus. Tell him whatever's on your heart right now, and then I'll close the prayer. (Allow time.)

PRAY Dear Jesus, you've given us eyes to see, and we want to see you clearly. We admit it's sometimes a struggle to see who you really are. Thank you for giving us your Word to offer a more accurate picture of you—and ourselves. Continue to refine and clarify our understanding of how you see us and how we see you. In Jesus' name, amen.

10. JESUS FEEDS US

Supplies: Bibles, the words to Ephesians 2:10 printed on slips of paper

ASK What's the biggest event, movement, or effort you've ever been part of, and how did it make you feel? (Allow time for sharing.)

Have students take turns reading John 6:1-13, about the boy and his lunch.

ASK How do you think the boy might've reacted when Andrew pointed him out? If you were that boy, what might you have been thinking and feeling when everyone was full and extra food remained?

SAY Let's take a few minutes to think about what Jesus has done in and through us in the past.

ASK What has Jesus done with your talents, abilities, gifts, willingness to serve, or any other part of you? How do you feel when you know Jesus has accomplished something cool through you?

Have someone read aloud Ephesians 2:10.

SAY God made us, in Christ, to do good things that he has already planned for us.

ASK Which part of that Bible verse is most meaningful to you and why? What's it like to know that Jesus has big plans for you—even though you might not know those plans yet? How willing are you to be part of whatever God created you to do?

Hand out slips of paper with the words to Ephesians 2:10.

SAY Let's have a time of prayer, where we each pray a first-person version of Ephesians 2:10. I'll start, and we'll go around to my left.

Close by having each person read the following words out loud as a prayer: *I am God's masterpiece. He has created me anew in Jesus so I can do the good things he planned for me long ago.*

11. JESUS GIVES US LIFE

Supplies: Bibles, paper, pen or pencil

[SAY] Open your Bibles to John 5:15, and let's read that verse together: "Yes, I am the vine; you are the branches. Those who remain in me, and I in them, will produce much fruit. For apart from me you can do nothing."

[SAY] Today's teenagers have been called the most connected generation in history. Do you think that's true? Why or why not? Let's make a quick list. In what ways, and to what things, people, or groups, do you feel connected?

Have someone keep a list. After everyone has shared, have that person read the list back.

[ASK] With all that "connection," do you ever feel unconnected or disconnected? Turn to a partner and discuss that for a minute. (Allow time.)

[SAY] I'd like you to consider one more question, and each partner will answer it briefly. There isn't a right answer or a "good, Sunday school" answer you're supposed to give. Thinking of all we've just shared, what's the most important connection for you? (Allow time.)

Have someone read aloud 1 John 5:12.

[ASK] How does the truth in that Bible verse make you feel about the connection that's most important to you?

[SAY] The great thing about being connected to Jesus is that he offers us life. When we're cut off from Jesus, we can't thrive or grow or do anything. Like a branch, we need to remain connected to the vine to live.

[SAY] Let's ask Jesus to bring his life, power, and love into every connection we have. Dear Jesus, thanks for being willing to connect to us so we can have life through you. Help us share that life-changing connection with other people we encounter. In Jesus' name, amen.

SECTION 3:

HOW DOES JESUS HELP US?

12. JESUS HELPS US OVERCOME FEAR

Supplies: Bibles

Have students take turns reading aloud Mark 4:35-40, the Bible passage about Jesus calming the storm.

ASK In this passage, what do you think Jesus stood for?

SAY It's okay to be afraid, but we have to remember that Jesus is standing with us through our fears. We also can stand with one another as we deal with fears, offering reminders of Jesus' presence and our support.

SAY Let's talk a bit more about our fears.

ASK If Jesus were here and asked you, "Why are you afraid?" what would you say? What in life makes you the most afraid? Why do you think it's so difficult to get past your greatest fears?

SAY Turn to a partner and tell about a time you depended on Jesus to get you through a difficult situation. (Allow time.)

ASK What's one way you can remember that Jesus is with you when you're dealing with fear?

SAY Thanks for being willing to share. Digging into feelings such as fear can be difficult. But allowing fear to control us or boss us around keeps us from living a full life with Jesus. So hang in there, and remember that Jesus is always with you. No matter what happens, you can give your fears to him.

SAY Let's close in prayer by turning to a new partner and taking one minute each to pray for the other person. Share one of your fears and then pray for each other, that Jesus will calm that fear with his presence.

Allow time for prayer.

13. JESUS HELPS US OVERCOME DOUBT

Supplies: Bibles

[SAY] I'm curious: What do you doubt about the Bible, our church, or your own faith in Jesus? Allow time, and then ask a few students to share their doubts. (Don't try to make this a time of answering the doubts; it's just about sharing them.)

[SAY] I want you to know it's okay to doubt. Jesus didn't condemn people for doubting, and neither will we.

Have someone read aloud Luke 24:35-40.

[ASK] When it comes to people in the Bible who doubted, how did Jesus react? What did he stand for?

[SAY] One way our doubts can be reassured is through words. They may not answer every doubt and question you have, but they can let you know that Jesus is real and that other people are standing with you in times of doubt. Sometimes, another person's words can help bridge the gap between doubting and quitting. Let's take some time to do this for each other.

[SAY] In a moment, we'll have a brief time of prayer where we ask Jesus to give us some special words for someone else in our group. After some silence, I'll let the rest of our time be open. If you have something you think Jesus wants you to share with another person here, simply speak it out in a sentence or two. It can be an encouragement, a compliment, or something else about how Jesus is working in that person's life. Let's keep it positive and not include any private or personal information. Please join me in praying:

After a brief silence, pray: Jesus, we all have doubts. Please give us words of encouragement to offer our friends—words that let us know you hear our doubts and we aren't alone. Thanks, Jesus. Amen.

Spend time sharing brief words of encouragement within your group. Don't be afraid of a little silence. When the sharing has ended, close in prayer.

14. JESUS HEALS US

Supplies: Bibles

Have students take turns reading aloud John 5:1-9.

ASK What did Jesus stand for in today's Bible passage? Think of some things you've needed Jesus' healing for. How has he responded to your requests? In what other ways does Jesus need to make you well?

SAY What Jesus did for us by dying on the cross and rising from the dead makes "getting well" possible. You don't have to do anything, fix anything, or become anything. Jesus did all that for you. He gave up his own "wellness," so to speak, so he could give it to you. We can respond to Jesus through our faith in him. But first, Jesus asks a question.

Have someone read aloud John 5:6.

ASK Why might someone resist being made well, either physically or spiritually?

SAY By believing in Jesus, we receive his ultimate healing, the gift of eternal life. We'll also have new, perfectly healed bodies in heaven—all because of what Jesus did for us.

Have someone read aloud 2 Corinthians 5:1.

ASK How does it feel to know that Jesus provides healing? What impact can that message of healing have on your life? on other people's lives? How can you share it with them?

SAY Close your eyes, and let's end with a time of prayer. If you have a new—or renewed—perspective on your relationship with Jesus, offer this simple prayer: "Jesus, I want to get well." You can go into more detail if you'd like, but there's no pressure to do that. After we've prayed for a while, I'll close. Let's bow our heads and pray.

Allow plenty of time for this to develop.

15. JESUS UNDERSTANDS US

Supplies: Bibles, paper, pens or pencils

[SAY] Listen to this story that illustrates how we sometimes forget that Jesus already understands us very well:

After his freshman year of college, a young man decided to get a summer job as a camp counselor. He'd never really spent a lot of time at camps, so his first week serving and leading kids was a revelation. He was responsible for eight kids—getting them to meals on time, helping them with camp activities, and supervising their bedtime. Getting everyone to quiet down after lights-out was an especially tough job.

Midway through the week, the young man called his mother, who'd raised six children, and excitedly shared his experiences. "Mom," he said, "you have no idea how hard it is to take care of all these kids. I have to get them up in the morning, take them to breakfast, be responsible for them all day...."

Mid-sentence, it occurred to the young man who he was addressing. He paused, with some embarrassment, and then sheepishly continued, "Well, maybe you do understand...."

His mother quietly chuckled on the other end of the line.

[SAY] Can you relate to this guy at all? Maybe you sometimes wonder, "How can Jesus really understand my reality? Nobody could understand it. I can't even understand it."

Hand out paper and pencils.

[SAY] Let's take some time to better understand Jesus' life experience. What is his reality like? Form three groups, and I'll give you each a Bible passage that describes what Jesus experienced firsthand. After reading the passage, talk about it. What happened to Jesus, and what was the experience like for him? One person should take notes. When I call you back, designate someone to share what you've learned about Jesus. (Explain that the Isaiah passage is a prophecy about Jesus from the Old Testament.)

- Group 1: Isaiah 53:2-8
- Group 2: Matthew 13:53-58
- Group 3: Matthew 26:69-74

Allow time for students to explore their Bible passage and take notes.

SAY Let's hear what you learned about Jesus from these Bible passages. We'll start with Group 1. (Allow time.)

SAY Jesus was falsely accused, criticized by people in his hometown and by his own family, rejected by his closest friends, physically abused, and ultimately killed. Wow! But I'll admit, when I'm having a really bad day I sometimes tell myself that Jesus can't possibly understand what I'm going through.

SAY Like that young man who called his mother, let's stop for our own "wait a minute" moment. I'll close this time with prayer. After the prayer, remain silent for a full minute and consider some things in your life that you've assumed Jesus wouldn't understand. Write those things down, and also jot down an experience Jesus had that reminds you he does understand your present situation.

PRAY Lord, some things in my life are really hard for me. Sometimes I wonder where you are and if you really understand how hard life gets. I'm so thankful for the experiences you had, Jesus; they remind me I'm not the only one who goes through rough times. Whenever I'm struggling, Jesus, help me remember that you get it. And help me remember you're here with me—even in the middle of the mess my life sometimes can be. Thank you for always being there, and for knowing the deepest parts of me. In your name, amen.

Have a minute of silence before ending the devotion.

16. JESUS FORGIVES US

Supplies: Bibles

SAY Is it really possible for us to find freedom and forgiveness from the things we regret? We want to believe that Jesus can do everything he promises to do, but a voice inside us often loops back around to remind us that our flaws, mistakes, and sins still impact us.

SAY I'll read a few short scenarios that'll get us thinking about the consequences of our mistakes and poor choices. After each one, we'll take a few minutes to discuss a question. Here's the first one: "Aaron is driving to school when his girlfriend texts, asking him to pick her up on his way. While responding to her text, he rams into the back of a car that's stopped at a light. The other driver is seriously injured, but Aaron is not."

ASK Which is harder: forgiving someone for hurting you or forgiving yourself for hurting someone? Explain. (Allow time.)

SAY Here's the second scenario: "Sydney loves Snapchat and sends pictures to her friends all the time. When she starts dating Tony, he keeps begging her to start sexting. Sydney doesn't want to at first, but Tony convinces her it's no big deal. Besides, nothing lasts more than 10 seconds on Snapchat. Finally, she decides it's okay."

ASK Once you've crossed a line and done something you can never take back, how is it even possible to have the freedom Jesus promises? (Allow time.)

SAY Here's the last scenario: "Zach doesn't like the new kid at school. Something about him is annoying. And the kid needs to know his place. So Zach starts posting nasty rumors, saying the kid had been kicked out of his previous school for drugs. Zach makes up one terrible story after another and gets his friends to share them online. Word of Zach's cyberbullying gets back to the school, and Zach is suspended."

ASK After doing something wrong, it's hard to resolve the tension between what we've done and the person we think we are. Think about how Jesus interacted with Peter after Peter had betrayed him. Based on that encounter, what do you know about Jesus' heart toward us when we screw up? (Allow time.)

SAY We can't go back and change the past. And when Jesus reframes our past, that doesn't mean the bad stuff we've done or the hurtful choices we've made will disappear. They're all still part of our past. Forgiveness means giving up all hope of a better past. Jesus reframes our past not by making it go away but by saying our past doesn't define who we are.

SAY I'll close in prayer now, and in the moments of silence, allow God to set you free from your past.

PRAY Lord, the freedom you've given us in Jesus is amazing. Thank you for the opportunity to let go of past hurts and bad choices. (Silence.) Thank you for reframing our past by removing all the shame, guilt, and pain—and for giving us a clean slate. (Silence.) Thank you for freeing us to be more like Jesus. Show us how we can live differently. (Silence.) In Jesus' name, amen.

28

JESUS CENTERED

YOUTH
GROUP
DEVOTIONS

PROVEN IMPACT WITH 100,000+ TEENAGERS

SECTION 4:

HOW IS JESUS RELEVANT TO OUR DAILY LIVES?

17. JESUS STRENGTHENS US

Supplies: Bibles

Have someone read aloud 2 Timothy 2:11-12.

ASK Does that Bible passage make you feel encouraged or discouraged, and why? What might be very, very difficult for you to endure for Jesus?

SAY Remaining is really the act of hanging in there. It's almost not an action at all but a state of waiting to do whatever will happen next. When we remain with Jesus, we're saying, "Jesus, I believe you…no matter what. So I'll wait." That's easy to say but really hard to do.

Have someone read aloud 1 John 2:24-25.

ASK What's the most difficult thing for you to believe about Jesus?

Have everyone open their Bibles to John 15:5. Read that verse aloud together.

ASK When, if ever, do you think it's difficult for Jesus to keep remaining with you? Explain.

SAY Jesus has remained with you since the beginning. It's incredible to realize that Jesus will always remain with you. He'll never quit…never abandon you…never write you off. And that can give you the strength and encouragement you need to remain with Jesus, even in the hardest of times.

Read aloud Hebrews 12:3.

SAY Let's close in prayer. I'll give you three things to pray about for one minute each. At the end of each minute of silent prayer, we'll all join together, praying, "Jesus, help us remain with you." Please bow your heads. First, take one minute and ask Jesus to bring to your mind the area of your life where you struggle the most to remain with him. (Allow one full minute.)

SAY Please pray with me, "Jesus, help us remain with you." Next, take one minute and thank Jesus for remaining with you through some of your most difficult times. Talk to Jesus about those times. (Allow one full minute.)

SAY Please pray with me, "Jesus, help us remain with you."

SAY Finally, take one minute and pray silently and specifically for one person in this room, asking Jesus to give him or her strength to remain. (Allow one full minute.)

SAY Please pray with me, "Jesus, help us remain with you. Amen."

18. JESUS RESTORES OUR RELATIONSHIPS

Supplies: Bibles, paper, pens or pencils, envelopes, stamps

SAY God, our heavenly Father, is the best parent we could ever have. He's a dream-parent, so to speak, loving each of his children (us!) more than we can imagine. And he put us together with other people we call our family. But because all earthly families consist of imperfect people, families experience conflict from time to time.

ASK During times of unresolved conflict, how has God responded to or helped you and your family?

SAY Just as God wants us to experience a restored relationship with him, he also wants our families to make things right—with one another and with him. Sometimes, families face a lot of hurt, pain, frustration, and grief. And when tough emotions go unspoken, forgiveness usually can't enter the picture. Other times, words we should say—moments of truth and honesty, or even a confession or apology—never get spoken because the time doesn't seem right.

ASK What do you need to say or write to someone in your family? Let's take some time right now to write a letter to a family member. It's up to you whether that letter gets delivered or not, so share whatever you're comfortable with.

Hand out paper, pens or pencils, and envelopes.

SAY Here's how we'll do this:

- What you write is personal. No one else in our group will read it.
- The letter can be to anyone in your family, or even a group of people.
- The letter can be short, long, or anywhere in between.
- You can share an apology, a regret, or even words of truth. Or you can offer forgiveness to a family member for something they've done to you.

- When you're finished, put the letter in your envelope. If you know the address and fill out the envelope, I'll mail these tomorrow. Or you can deliver the letter in person.
- If you're dealing with some tough issues, we're here for you. Come see me afterward to talk.

Allow about 10 minutes for letter-writing.

ASK How do you think your family member will respond to what he or she reads? How might this letter be a first step in restoring or strengthening your relationship?

Close in prayer, thanking Jesus for our families and for helping restore our relationships with family members. Remember to stamp and mail any letters.

19. JESUS RELATES TO OUR EMOTIONS

Supplies: Bibles

[SAY] Turn to a person next to you and share—if you're willing—one thing you're frustrated or angry with Jesus about. Take about one minute each. (Allow time.)

[ASK] Does anyone want to share your thoughts with the whole group? There's no pressure, but this is a safe group of people to share your struggles with. (Allow time for young people to share their thoughts and struggles. Don't try to make this a time of answering the "whys" of what people are going through.)

[SAY] During his time on earth, Jesus faced intense emotions. Open your Bibles to John 11, and let's read about some of them.

Have students take turns reading aloud John 11:17-44.

[ASK] In verse 33, why do you think Jesus felt angry?

[ASK] How do you think Lazarus' family felt after Jesus brought him back to life? How satisfied do you think they were with how Jesus handled things?

[ASK] If Jesus showed up today and fixed whatever is making you most frustrated or angry with him, do you think you'd forgive and forget quickly, or would it take a while? Explain.

[ASK] How does your answer affect how much hope and comfort you can take from the Lazarus story we just read? In other words, can you receive hope and comfort from Jesus if you're angry with him? Why or why not?

[SAY] In a moment, I'll ask you to reflect on some words from the Bible that I'll read to you. They're from 2 Thessalonians 2:16-17, and they're an encouragement, a prayer, and a blessing. Please bow your heads with me.

[SAY] Jesus, just like Mary and Martha, we can only trust that you are who you say you are. We can only trust that you love us today like you did when you died for us. We can only hope that you will save the day for us, Jesus. Help us share our feelings and frustrations with you, but never let them stop us from walking and talking with you. You are our hope, Jesus. We know that because of these words from 2 Thessalonians 2:16: "Now may our Lord Jesus Christ himself and God our Father, who loved us and by his grace gave us eternal comfort and a wonderful hope, comfort you and strengthen you in every good thing you do and say." Amen.

20. JESUS NURTURES OUR FAITH

Supplies: Bibles, paper and a pen or pencil for one person to take notes

Have students take turns reading aloud Acts 9:10-19.

[SAY] Even though Ananias feared for his safety and probably even his life, he made faith in Jesus his top priority. When Ananias obeyed God by going to Saul (who didn't like Christians, to say the least), God used him to restore Saul's sight. Ananias literally put his hands on a man who might kill him. He became a story of transformation.

[ASK] When you think about living your faith in Jesus, what makes you fearful: what others think of you? doubts about yourself? the risk of standing up for your faith? being the person you know you should be but are afraid to become? something else? Go around and have students each share a brief answer, if they're willing.

[SAY] Turn to a person next to you and pray briefly for his or her fear. If you can't remember exactly what they said, just ask. Take one minute—30 seconds each—to pray for the fears of the person next to you. (Allow time for prayer.)

[SAY] Thanks for praying for each other. One way Jesus nurtures our faith is by giving us fellow Christians to lean on. That's why he put us in this group.

[ASK] What are some ways we can live out our faith together—especially when we face fears? Is Jesus giving us any ideas or thoughts about something we can do as a youth group, as small groups, or even as individuals?

Allow time for brainstorming and discussion. Don't get hung up on details. Have someone take notes. After many ideas have been shared, try to narrow down the list to two ideas that everyone agrees are doable.

[SAY] These are some great ideas. Thanks for sharing!

Appoint people to follow up with these ideas.

Close in prayer by reading aloud Psalm 34:4 several times: *I prayed to the Lord, and he answered me. He freed me from all my fears.*

21. JESUS HOLDS OUR FUTURE

Supplies: Bibles, paper, pens or pencils

[SAY] People aren't used to getting something they didn't pay for or earn. When we do undeserved, unexpected service in Jesus' name, that's really a glimpse of what Jesus did for us.

Have students open their Bibles to Luke 15.

[SAY] In the prodigal son parable, the father character is an amazing example of God's love and provision. Let's read some key verses about the father.

Read aloud verse 12, verse 20, verses 22-24, and verses 31-32.

[SAY] Let's keep those verses in mind as we discuss these questions:

- Throughout the story, did the father's response to both his sons change or stay the same? Why do you think that was the case?
- Do you feel that Jesus has treated you the same or differently throughout your relationship with him? Why?
- You may have heard that Jesus "deserves your best." Do you agree with that statement? Why or why not?

[SAY] If Jesus does deserve our best—just because of who he is and what he's done for us—that includes our future, which starts right now. Thinking about what lies ahead can be exciting as well as scary. But let's dream a little.

[ASK] What might your future look like if you let Jesus guide it 100 percent? (Pause.)

[ASK] What things are stopping you from letting Jesus do that? (Pause.)

[SAY] Take a few minutes and list anything and everything you can think of that makes you afraid to trust Jesus as you head to your future. (Allow time.)

Ask if anyone is willing to share some items they wrote.

ASK If you set aside those fears and obstacles, what's the biggest, coolest, most amazing thing you can see Jesus doing in your future? Do you think you can allow Jesus to be in control of some of your future? all of your future? Explain.

Close in prayer, thanking Jesus for holding our future and asking him to renew our trust in him.

22. JESUS MAKES EVERYTHING NEW

Supplies: Bibles, rags or scraps of cloth (two per person), markers, a trash bag

SAY If you've ever tackled a really tough load of laundry, you know stains can be stubborn. Sometimes even the best stain remover fails to make dirty clothes truly clean again. That's how it can feel when we mess up and don't live as Jesus wants us to.

Give each student one rag and a marker.

SAY Take a few minutes to think about some things that make you feel soiled inside. These can be things you shouldn't have done or things you should've done. You don't need to share them with anyone, and you can use code words or drawings, if you'd like. (Allow time.)

ASK Looking at your dirty rag, how does it make you feel? Do you think anything could make that rag clean again?

Hold up a trash bag. Have students take turns dropping their dirty rags inside. Then tie the bag shut tightly.

Give each student a new, clean rag.

ASK What was it like to give up your old, dirty rag? What was it like to receive a new, clean one? How is that like what Jesus does for us?

SAY What Jesus did for you and me through his death on the cross and resurrection from the dead makes "everything new" possible. You don't have to do anything, fix anything, or become anything. Jesus did it for you. He has already made everything new for you. You only need to respond to Jesus in faith. That's summed up by Jesus' own words in John 6:47. Will someone please read that Bible verse? (Allow time.)

SAY That's my prayer for you—that you'll believe in Jesus, who offers new life.

SAY Let's close in a time of open prayer. If you have a new—or renewed—perspective on your relationship with Jesus, offer this simple prayer: "Jesus, thanks for making me new." You can go into more detail if you'd like. After we've prayed for a while, I'll close. Let's bow our heads and pray.

Allow plenty of time for this to develop. Don't be afraid of silence.

28

JESUS
CENTERED

YOUTH
GROUP
DEVOTIONS

PROVEN IMPACT WITH 100,000+ TEENAGERS

SECTION 5:

WHAT DOES IT MEAN TO FOLLOW JESUS?

23. JESUS TRANSFORMS US

Supplies: Bibles, paper, pens or pencils

Have students take turns reading aloud Mark 5:1-20.

ASK What's the most surprising part of this Bible passage, and why?

SAY This is quite a transformational story. It's interesting to note that the man possessed by the evil spirit actually ran toward Jesus so Jesus could transform him.

ASK What's the farthest you've ever run (or jogged, or even walked), and why were you doing it? If you had to either run toward $5 million or run away from five years of sorrow, which would you choose? If you had to either run toward a lifetime of unknown adventure or run toward a lifetime of predictable safety, which would you choose?

SAY Being transformed involves the new and unknown. But that's where Jesus wants us to run—toward a new life with him.

ASK Do you think you generally run toward Jesus or away from him? Explain.

SAY Running toward someone who can help you is more valuable than merely running away from something bad. But you have to know and trust the person you're running to. In a moment, I'm going to ask you to take a three-minute walk by yourself. (Stay nearby, even if you have to walk in circles!) During that time, imagine that you're walking or even running toward Jesus. Ask him to show you why you need to run to him. Is there a situation where Jesus can give you protection? Someone who maybe shouldn't be influencing you but is? A personal struggle you can take to Jesus? Or anything else. Ready? Walk!

After about three minutes, gather everyone back together. Hand out paper and pens or pencils.

SAY Now take a few minutes to write down whatever came to mind. Make a list of reasons to run to Jesus. (Allow time.)

SAY Be encouraged! Jesus wants you to know the truth about how much he loves you, and he wants to transform your life for the best.

Close in prayer by reading Proverbs 18:10 and asking Jesus to remind you to keep running toward him to receive his transformation.

24. JESUS EMBRACES US

Supplies: Bibles

Have students take turns reading aloud Luke 19:1-10.

SAY Zacchaeus—often known as a "wee little man"—was a pretty rotten person and certainly not a Christ-follower. But the Bible tells us that after one meal with Jesus, salvation came to Zacchaeus' house that day. In other words, Zacchaeus believed in Jesus right there. He was a sinner who embraced Jesus in order to experience transformation. Zacchaeus knew that would be costly, people would doubt his motives, and the outcome was uncertain at best. Yet, he still put everything on the line to embrace Jesus and have an encounter with God's Son.

SAY To make some comparisons, this would be like:

- a bank robber running into a courthouse to talk to the judge,
- an escaped prisoner knocking on the warden's door,
- a drug dealer rushing in to see the chief of police,

combined with…

- going to the haircut place, shutting your eyes, and saying, "Do whatever you want,"
- bungee jumping while blindfolded and having never looked down,
- ordering off a foreign-language menu of a place you've never been and food you've never eaten,

and don't forget…

- most people would be laughing or sneering at you,
- your "friends" would surely leave you behind, and
- you'd also lose your job.

ASK Turn to a partner and discuss this question: Which of the above phrases is the most intimidating to you personally, and why? (Allow time.)

SAY Getting to Jesus and embracing him can be very costly. It's one thing if Jesus bumps into us as we're living life. But when we drop everything to get to him, we're jumping in front of a moving train of repair and transformation. Part of what happens next is on us.

ASK What are some risks involved with embracing Jesus and pursuing the type of life he asks us to lead?

SAY Jesus embraced death on a cross so you can be transformed and have a new life. Zacchaeus gives us a real-life example of the simplicity of experiencing transformation by embracing Christ.

Form a circle and "embrace" one another by holding hands. Then close in prayer, thanking Jesus for embracing us so he can make us more like him.

25. JESUS PRODUCES FRUIT IN US

Supplies: Bibles, paper, pens or pencils

SAY When we follow Jesus and share his love, he can connect to other people through us. That's really cool.

Have someone read aloud John 15:8.

ASK How would you define the idea of producing or bearing "fruit" for Jesus?

SAY Being connected to Jesus, who calls himself the Vine, allows our lives to be fruitful for him.

ASK Turn to a partner and discuss these questions: What's one way you feel fruitful for Jesus? What's one area you need Jesus' help to produce more fruit for him?

ASK How can we as a group produce more fruit? To help figure that out, let's form two groups: Inside Fruit and Outside Fruit. We'll form the groups by going around and calling out "inside" or "outside." I'll start.

Form groups. Give each group paper and a pen or pencil.

SAY Our task is to come up with some very practical ways to produce much fruit. Inside people, come up with ways to produce much "inside fruit" in our youth ministry. Those are ways we can keep connecting more with Jesus in everything we do. They're ideas for us to remain in Jesus and let Jesus be more "in us." They can be devotional ideas, group activities, or anything that keeps us focused on our relationship with Jesus. Outside people, your job is to come up with ideas to produce much fruit outside our youth ministry. Those are things we can do for our families, friends, community, or even the world. Choose one person in your group to write down ideas. After five minutes, we'll come back together and share. (Allow time for brainstorming.)

SAY Let's hear the inside ideas. (Allow time for reporting, and ask for any additional ideas from the entire group.)

SAY And now the outside ideas. (Allow time for reporting, and ask for any additional ideas from the entire group.)

SAY Now, let's pick one inside and one outside idea that we'll commit to working on. Select the two ideas, appoint a few people to stay on top of them, and set a deadline.

Close in prayer, asking Jesus to produce fruit through each of you individually and through your entire group.

26. JESUS OPENS OUR EYES

Supplies: Bibles

Have students close their eyes while you read aloud Mark 8:22-26.

SAY In this Bible passage, Jesus healed a man of blindness. Interestingly, Jesus didn't want the man to return to his home village afterward. The point was this: Don't just return to your same old state of life. Go be different.

ASK What did Jesus want the blind man to stand for after he received his sight?

SAY Before we follow Jesus, our eyes are closed. We're blinded by sin, unable to see what Jesus has done for us—and how he wants us to live.

ASK As you've gotten to know Jesus and develop a relationship with him, how has he "opened your eyes"? What do you now see differently because you follow Jesus?

Have someone read aloud Psalm 119:18.

SAY We don't always associate God's laws or instructions with the word "wonderful." But it does contain eye-opening truths that keep us on the right path as we live a Jesus-centered life.

ASK Turn to a partner and discuss these questions: In what ways has God's Word opened your eyes about your need for a Savior? about what Jesus has done for you? about how to live for Jesus? (Allow time.)

Ask if anyone is willing to share their insights with the whole group.

SAY Let's form a circle and close in prayer. If you're willing, we'll each ask Jesus: "Open my eyes to _____." Fill in the blank however you'd like. When everyone's done, I'll close our prayer time.

Begin with your own prayer. Allow time. Be prepared to close in prayer when it seems like everyone who wants to has prayed.

27. JESUS SETS US FREE

Supplies: Bibles, paper, pens or pencils

ASK Think of a time you've felt set free. Maybe it was the last day of school or the end of a really big project. What types of emotions did you experience, and why?

Have someone read aloud Galatians 5:1.

SAY Following Jesus provides the best type of freedom imaginable because he sets us free from sin and death. But Jesus also sets us free *to* things.

ASK What things do you think Jesus sets us free *to*?

SAY Peter, one of Jesus' disciples, denied knowing Jesus as Jesus was being put on trial and crucified. Peter cowered and hid, fully aware he'd betrayed his best friend. Afterward, he went back to the fishing business he'd been running before he left it behind to follow Jesus. But after Jesus rose from the dead—setting all of us free—he seeks out Peter and his friends and calls them back from their fishing boat. Jesus calls them to a freedom that involves service to others.

Have students take turns reading aloud John 21:15-19.

ASK What does Jesus ask Peter to do on that beach? What if Jesus told you he had set you free in order to "feed his sheep"? How would you respond?

SAY Turn to a partner. Take a few minutes to discuss ways you already use your God-given freedom to serve Jesus and other people. (Allow time.)

SAY Now, with your partner, discuss some new or different ways you can use your freedom to serve Jesus and other people. (Allow time.)

SAY Because Jesus promises to always be with us, we aren't alone while choosing how to use the freedom he gives us. Knowing the heart of Jesus—and why he set us free—is important as we continue to follow him and serve others.

Close in prayer, thanking Jesus for setting us free to serve him and other people.

28. JESUS MAKES US CHANGE AGENTS

Supplies: Bibles, paper, pens or pencils

ASK How many of you like change? (Ask for a show of hands.) Why is change often scary? In what ways can change be good?

SAY Jesus is a "change agent" because his sacrifice on the cross made your life—and future—much better. Jesus transforms you, opens your eyes, and sets you free to serve him and others. In those ways, Jesus turns you into a change agent, too.

Have someone read aloud Romans 12:1-2.

ASK Knowing what Jesus did for you, how do you want to respond? Why is it tempting to continue to follow the patterns of this world? In your day-to-day life, how can you remember that Jesus has transformed you? How can you show that Jesus has transformed you?

SAY The types of changes Jesus makes in us—and wants us to keep making—are exciting. They allow us to worship Jesus by how we live each day.

SAY Turn to a partner and discuss some ways Jesus is using you as a change agent. (Allow time.)

Hand out paper and pens or pencils.

SAY Reflecting on the discussion you just had with your partner, choose one way you're a change agent for Jesus. On your paper, draw a badge and write "change agent" on it. Then add a word or two—or even a picture—to remind you about being a change agent for Jesus. Take the badge home and put it somewhere you'll see it often.

Close in prayer, thanking Jesus for changing us and for making us his change agents in the world.